My Healing Companion

Published by

Comeback Press, Inc.
PMB #246, 27 West Anapamu Street
Santa Barbara, CA 93101-3143
www.beverlykirkhart.com
comebackpress@cox.net
Toll Free: 1-866-431-0918

Library of Congress Number: 00-090403

ISBN-10: 0-9710425-0-0
ISBN-13: 978-0- 9710425-0-6

Special thanks to Jack Canfield, author of *Chicken Soup for the
Soul*, for his teaching of the strength wheel (page 117)
in his eight-day summer training program.

The purpose of this journal is to inspire and to educate.
The information found is not intended to be a substitute for
professional medical advice, diagnosis, or treatment.
Medical concerns or questions should be addressed
to your health care provider.

Book production coordinated by To Press and Beyond
www.topressandbeyond.com

Printed in the United States of America

My Healing Companion
was completed by

....

With help from my friend,

Beverly Katherine Kirkhart

To my mother,

Dorothy Ellen Smith,

who fought her cancer battle with dignity

and courage. Her indomitable spirit

will remain with me always.

My dear friend,

I am so pleased to be sharing *My Healing Companion* with you. I wrote in a journal just like this throughout my cancer journey. It provided a safe place to record my feelings and to begin loving my body and myself again.

Journaling helped me to become the person I am today. I hope that some of the activities in this book will help you or those closest to you meet your challenge with cancer.

In an odd but wonderful way, cancer changed my life for the better, and, I hope you, too, will make the same discovery.

All my love,
Beverly Katherine Kirkhart
Breast cancer survivor since 1993
Santa Barbara, California

Foreword

It began to seem as if every day I would hear that someone I knew, or a friend of a friend, had been diagnosed with cancer. Then one day that person everyone was talking about was me.

Like Beverly, my life was turned upside down. Everything else was put on hold, because, from the moment I was diagnosed with breast cancer, my new life was all about how to rid my body of this disease. And my attitude was simple: take my breasts if it will save my life. I was (and am) very clear about what is important.

The emotions and feelings that Beverly writes about—and encourages you to write about—in this journal were the types of emotions with which I had to deal. Yes, I kept a journal (I'm a JOURNALIST, for goodness' sake), but I wish I'd had this one, because it helps guide you through the journey and gives you ways to express yourself during what can be, no matter how many friends or how much family you have, a lonely time. Besides, I found that writing about the experience, even keeping notes on my feelings, mental and physical, helped me understand what I really WAS feeling.

My Healing Companion is not only a useful tool, it comes from someone who's been there, done that, and lived to tell the tale. Moreover, she's taken those experiences and put them together in this journal in such a way as to help you get to the heart of your own emotions.

Look, we all know good thoughts won't cure cancer. But you can help yourself in many ways. And this is one of them.

Put down in this journal what makes you happy, what makes you sad, who you can count on, what you need, what you're not getting, what you can draw on to get through your bout with cancer, what makes you laugh—and I assure you that if you're open to it, you will find laughter in the experience. You will find life worth living, even while going through cancer. After all, YOU ARE A SURVIVOR. Otherwise you wouldn't be reading this.

So welcome to the club you never wanted to join. You'll meet a lot of nice people in this club. You already know that, from the minute you were diagnosed with cancer, your life changed forever. Like Beverly and the thousands of others who have taken this disease head on, I believe what counts is enjoying the time you have, be it ten days or one hundred years—while you keep on fighting, for yourself, your sisters, and all our daughters.

Best of luck on your journey.

Linda Ellerbee
Breast cancer survivor since 1992

How This Journal Came About

*I*n 1991, my life fell apart. My marriage ended in a divorce, I was forced to file for bankruptcy, and my business and dream home vanished! As if that wasn't enough hardship, in October 1993, I was diagnosed with breast cancer. Hearing those words, "Beverly, your tumor is cancerous," was overwhelming and deeply terrifying. I was suddenly forced to stare death in the face, and to make major life decisions, alone and destitute.

Upon reflection, I realize that this was the moment when my new life emerged! I began a journey of self-discovery and uncovered a hidden inner strength. I summoned the courage to live, turning setbacks into comebacks. I became my own hero.

What helped me to survive my experience with cancer was a small book filled with empty pages. These blank pages symbolized my new life. I chose to determine how my new life would progress. I wrote often in these pages—about how I felt on the day I was diagnosed in the doctor's office. I wrote about how empowered I felt after deciding to challenge myself to complete the 100-Mile Century Bike Ride. When I was so moved, I opened my book and wrote about my childhood, and pasted in pictures of myself as a young girl—smiling, happy, and full of life!

I found journaling to be liberating and positive. It was a safe haven in which to express my deepest feelings and not feel judged, criticized, or analyzed. The more freely I wrote, the closer I got to my feelings, which helped me to express myself more clearly, accept my emotions, and experience an inner peace—giving me a quality of life I so desperately was seeking. To this day, I continue to read the words I wrote in My Healing Companion.

Now, this was not easy. At first, I avoided writing at all cost. In fact, I never kept a diary as a child. However, I discovered that once I began journaling, it was truly worth the effort—it far outweighed my reluctance to write!

We all face cancer differently. How you respond to your disease is up to you. You can choose how you move through your cancer journey. Writing in this journal is just one way, and it may not be the only way you confront your cancer. I found this method so valuable that I decided to share it with others.

I hope you will give it a try. You might not agree with everything I have written, but why not try it out? You may find comfort in the special thoughts and activities in your journal. Keeping a journal may help you get through each

day, face the tough issues, and possibly start a new life. I encourage you to make notes throughout your day. Briefly write down your thoughts, feelings, and/or insights that pop into your mind. Take your journal with you to your doctors' visits and treatments. During quiet times, elaborate upon your thoughts, feelings, and/or experiences in blank pages. Think of your journal as a close friend, encouraging you to find strength, and inviting you on a journey that may lead to new adventures. Within this journal, you will become your own hero. As your friend and companion, you are not alone. I'll be traveling with you on your cancer journey.

Write

Write

Write

Write

*I write entirely
to find out what I'm thinking,
what I'm looking at,
what I see and what it means.
What I want and what I fear.*

—Joan Didion

Write to Survive

*Y*our written words are your best friend. You want to treasure them forever, like precious jewels.

Imagine holding a diamond in its natural rough form. There is no luster, but you know you are holding a precious commodity, so you work hard to cut, shape, and shine this jewel. Over time your hard work pays off—a twinkle of light shines from your hand. As you hold it up, the sun creates an array of glowing colors. You're in awe of its beauty. Your wonderment of this diamond's splendor is confirmed; in your hand is a precious stone you will treasure forever.

I use this analogy because it is similar to keeping a journal. When you record your thoughts in a journal you are unlocking the true brilliance of your inner strength and beauty. The more you let the pen flow on paper, the more you begin to uncover the real luster of your heart, which radiates from the inside out!

Journaling is a powerful tool for your emotional healing no matter what you may be facing, whether you are a patient, a loved one caring for a survivor, or a medical professional. Recent studies have shown that the benefits of expressive writing help to reduce stress, lessen doctor visits, and increase the immune system. I have all types of cancer patients who journal: prostrate patients, young breast cancer survivors, mothers and their daughters, and husband and wife teams journaling together. In addition, there are oncology nurses who meet once a month for a journal session to let out their feelings of loss, anger, and sadness.

Journaling can be fun, easy, and rewarding! You might be saying to yourself, where am I going to find the time; I hate to write; I can't spell. These are all valid reasons why you may not keep a journal. But I've written this book to help you overcome your reluctance to journal. *My Healing Companion* is a self-directed journal to guide you through the writing process. It will help you cope with your emotions of a cancer diagnosis and emerge as a stronger more positive person.

The following are simple tips to help you get started with the journaling adventure.

How to Keep a Journal

Find the specific time of the day that best works for you, and build it into your schedule just like a business or doctor's appointment. And don't let anything but emergencies interfere or pull you away. Also, don't say no to an urge to write at anytime. Give yourself the freedom to jot down your thoughts whenever they occur.

Find a place to write that is comforting, relaxing, and peaceful. Perhaps it's a room in your house, or your patio, or the library, or your favorite coffee shop.

Create a stimulating environment. What turns you on? Is it music? Burning candles? The aroma of a cup of tea or espresso? For me, it was turning on a soothing tape and writing by candlelight.

What to write on? If you don't have a copy of *My Healing Companion*, think about investing in one of the bound journals now available at many bookstores or stationary departments. If a thought occurs, grab a piece of paper or napkin, and write!

What to write with? Any pen will do, but consider treating yourself to a quality writing instrument that you only use for journal writing. One woman told me that she spent sixty-five dollars on a pen, but it made her happier than ever to write.

Date every entry. It helps to reference your thoughts. You might want to go back and read what you wrote for your own purpose, or for someone else who is facing a similar situation.

Write what's on your mind. Give yourself permission to let your thoughts flow out on paper with whatever method you choose. To unleash your thoughts, feel free to express your writing in any way that works for you. If you're happy, consider writing in pink ink. If you're sad, try blue ink. Also, write big, write small, from left to right, in a circle, whatever your mood dictates. If you can't find the words, draw a picture. Let the child in you roam free, and your spirits will follow. If your thoughts are documented in e-mails, print them out and save them in a folder or three-ring binder.

Don't edit yourself. We already spend too much time judging ourselves. Trusting yourself means giving your feelings full rein to come out. So who cares if you misspell a word or don't write complete sentences! It's your journal—and no one will ever see it—unless you want them to.

Now that you have an understanding of the benefits of journaling and how to get started, you are ready to put pen to paper and discover the treasures of your inner strength, beauty, and wisdom!

Why? Why? Why? Why? Why?

Some people look
At the world and say
"why."
Some people look at
the world and say
"why not?"

—George Bernard Shaw

Why Me?

*T*he test results are in and your doctor delivers the news, "You have cancer." Your world stops; it's silent. You are shocked, frightened, disbelieving, frozen in a vision of death. You wonder if this is a dream. *No, it can't be happening to me*, you think, as fear sets in. You pray for someone to take the fear away, but no one can. This is your battle, your challenge, your lesson in life. You may choose to remain in the *why me?* victim role or move into a spirit of *why not me?*

In 1993, as I was going through a divorce and bankruptcy, my life was in turmoil. I was under tremendous stress. Everything seemed to be out of control. I was emotionally drained. I couldn't think clearly, and I was numb to my feelings. These were all signs that something was dreadfully wrong.

Each day was a struggle. I dragged my lifeless body out of bed and forced myself to face the daunting issues before me. Then, one September morning, as I was showering, I felt the lump. My heart sank and terror struck, shaking my body to the core.

Immediately, I was referred to a surgeon who took a biopsy. After waiting three painfully long days, the reports came in. The surgeon delivered the bad news. It was an aggressive cancerous tumor, and I had a 40 percent chance of survival. The memories of my mother dying a slow death clouded my mind. I feared cancer because my family had a long history with this disease and many did not survive.

Stiff with fear, I walked out of the doctor's office, crawled into my friend's car, and broke down. I let go, shedding oceans of tears. In between my sobs and gasps, I cried out, "Why me? I'm too young to die! Haven't I dealt with enough crap?" I felt rejected and undesirable. I felt like I was facing a death sentence. And I felt very alone.

I was consumed with anger, depression. I acted out the victim role and fell desperately into the black hole of self-pity. What I needed was the confidence and higher self-esteem necessary to bravely face my cancer challenge.

How do you begin to raise your self-esteem, let go of *why me?* and live the spirit of *why not me?* I believe it starts with loving yourself. Have you forgotten your unique qualities—those special traits that make you the extraordinary person you are today?

I would have remained a victim if I hadn't seen Deb, a longtime friend, at the the Cancer Center of Santa Barbara. Deb was facing her own challenge of ovarian cancer. Each month, she went to the hospital for heavy daylong doses of chemotherapy. Deb became my mentor. In her wisdom, she spoke of how she regained her self-esteem in the face of cancer. Her words resonated in my soul. "You will live. You simply must believe in yourself!" These powerful words became my lifeline. I grabbed the rope and began pulling myself up, slowly, hand over hand, until I came out of my deep black hole of self-pity.

It took another survivor to make me realize it was my responsibility to believe in myself. As my self-confidence grew, my attitude toward cancer changed. I didn't want to be a victim any longer.

Can you think of a point in your life where you changed from victim to victor?

Think back to when you were a child; maybe you stood up to the class bully, or you said "no" to peer pressure.

Did you face insurmountable odds and have to take control of the situation to survive? The same actions you used then, beating the odds, taking a stance for yourself, are the skills you can use to deal with your cancer today.

Take a few minutes right now to jot down your thoughts.

POSITIVE TURNING POINTS IN MY LIFE

POSITIVE TURNING POINTS IN MY LIFE

Deb helped me make a commitment to myself that I wanted to LIVE. But did I want to live with low self-esteem? NO! Out of frustration, I wrote down words that I felt described who I was. I wrote them on Post-Its and stuck them all over my house. Every time I walked by a Post-It, I said aloud: "I'm dependable." "I'm a good friend." "I am resilient."

What Are Your Best Qualities?

Grab a pen, pencil, or crayon and start listing your best qualities. You may surprise yourself when you find out how much you have to offer yourself and others.

To get you started, below are some that I came up with.

I am smart

I am brave!

I am a whole person!

My bald head is beautiful!

I "DO" make a difference!

The following are examples of personal strengths. Can you add to this list? I encourage you to take 5 minutes and write down some of your best qualities on the next page.

Artistic	Good friend	Loving parent
Bright	Dedicated to my job	Encourages others
Brave	Sense of humor	Helpful
Compassionate	Responsible	Organized
Communicates well	Quick learner	Team player
Excellent cook	Physically fit	Trusting
Honest	Good with my hands	Makes a difference

MY BEST QUALITIES

MY BEST QUALITIES

I discovered that positive affirmations were a must for me. I cherished handwritten notes, greeting cards, and comments written in my journal. Another survivor suggested saving get-well cards. She discovered that by rereading the uplifting comments, she found hope, courage, and inspiration.

I reached out to my medical team and they came through. The following is a quote from Mary, one of my oncology nurses. I embraced her words and they became my lifeline to survival.

"Beverly, it is an honor caring for you. Because of who you are, I'm a better nurse, mother, wife, and human being. . . . Thank you for giving me the opportunity to care for you."

—Love, Mary

I know you're already feeling better about yourself. Let who you are shine!

Positive Words Offered by Others

Ask your caregivers and medical team, who are most familiar with you, to jot down what they admire about you. Explain to them how important it is to gain their support in order to maintain a positive outlook. Flash your irresistible smile, hand them a pen, along with your journal, and let them acknowledge you. You will regain awareness of how special and gifted you truly are, and, with higher self-esteem, you may have the confidence to ask, *why not me?*

POSITIVE WORDS FROM THOSE CLOSE TO ME

Positive Words from Those Close to Me

POSITIVE WORDS FROM THOSE CLOSE TO ME

Positive Words from Those Close to Me

PRIVATE THOUGHTS

PRIVATE THOUGHTS

PRIVATE THOUGHTS

PRIVATE THOUGHTS

ANGER

Anger

Anger

Anger

You can't keep misery
from coming
but you
don't have to give it
a chair to sit on.

—A Proverb

I'm Overwhelmed by Anger

Anger is the best word to describe how I felt about my cancer. I resented women who had hair, perfect bodies, and children—things I felt cancer had robbed me of.

I was overwhelmed with anger and the burden of acting like the perfect victim-patient-survivor. I believed family and friends expected me to be courageous, upbeat, and positive. This left me with no outlet for grief or anger, so I remained silent, mad, and resentful for several months after my diagnosis.

I lost my husband to a divorce, lost my business and home to bankruptcy, and now I have lost my health to cancer . . . I have a right to be angry at everything and everyone!

Beverly Kirkhart, Journal Entry, Dec. 6, 1993

It's normal to be angry, and sometimes you can use that anger to your advantage. Directed properly, it can be a powerful motivator to help you overcome insurmountable challenges. I have met many individuals who use their anger to fuel their drive to get well. Allow a time to express your anger, but schedule it—like an appointment—so there is a time to stop as well. Constant anger is not healthy. Negative thoughts rob energy and strength, weakening the immune system.

There is no right or wrong way to deal with your anger. Each one of us handles anger differently. The key to making it work for you is to acknowledge and express it. You are honoring yourself and your experience. Clearing anger out of your mental closet makes room for healing images that will nourish and restore you.

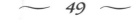

Here's how I recognized and came to grips with my anger.

I had done my homework. I knew the facts about my disease and the options for treatment. After thoroughly researching the pros and cons of chemotherapy, I elected this form of therapy. Knowledge helped replace some of my fears, but it did not begin to assuage my anger.

I was bitter, resentful, and negative as I entered the cancer clinic that gloomy Friday in November, for my first round of chemotherapy. A friendly nurse greeted me and kindly showed me down the hall to the chemo room. Once there, I told her in no uncertain terms how furious I was about taking toxic drugs for a disease I shouldn't have in the first place.

The nurse gently tried to calm me down as she injected the drugs into my veins. I felt the cold liquid flow through my right arm as it began its destructive journey throughout my body. I was tense, unhappy, and irate as I sat in the chemo chair, counting every second until I could get out of there. When my dosage was complete, 10,800 seconds later, I raced out of the clinic as furious as when I arrived, and stayed that way for the rest of the day.

As evening wore on, side effects hit me like a Mack truck: vomiting, constipation, sweating, fever-like flu. The only thing I could do was cry. During the night, which crept by so slowly I thought it would never end, I lay in bed exhausted, floating in and out of a light sleep. At morning light, it occurred to me my violent reaction to the chemotherapy was probably partly because of my angry attitude. I realized, and believe to this day, that my body was sending me a message: Let go of those hateful and angry emotions.

I was determined never again to experience such a horrible reaction. Prior to my second treatment, I talked to my nurse and researched techniques to help me release my hateful attitude, address my fear of death and find peace in my situation.

I faithfully practiced these methods, which helped me move through my healing process.

Meditation:

The act of quieting my mind.

Visualization:

I visualized the chemotherapy as white light surrounding and flushing the black cancer cells out of my body.

Beach walks:

Breathing in the healing ocean air.

Here are things you can do every day to stay calm. Practice them.

Deep breathing—slowly breathe in, filling up your stomach, then your lungs. Release through your mouth.

Pray or meditate.

Exercise.

Listen to music.

Distract yourself with a hobby.

Go out into nature.

Journaling: Explore your deepest emotions and write them down.

Take a moment to reflect back on a time when you were really angry at something or someone but you were not willing to acknowledge or voice this anger; as a result, the situation got worse. Write down your experience in the following space.

Do you see any benefits in staying angry?

On the next few pages, jot down your responses to these questions and flush out your anger, sadness, and fear.

Why do I hide my true feelings?

Why am I angry?

Who makes me angry and why?

How does my anger make me feel?

What am I afraid of?

On a scale of 1–10, how angry do I feel?

Under what circumstances do I get most angry?

Do I frighten others and myself when I get angry?

How can I resolve my anger?

Why does my sadness hurt so deeply?

MY ANGER, SADNESS, AND FEARS

My Anger, Sadness, and Fears

MY ANGER, SADNESS, AND FEARS

I found that a healing letter was and still is extremely helpful in all areas of my life—relationships, professional, and personal.

This letter involves six stages: Anger and resentment, hurt, fear, remorse and regret, wants, and love, compassion, forgiveness, and appreciation.

Here is an excerpt from one of my healing letters:

Write a healing letter to yourself.

Find a peaceful spot. This could be your favorite room, a coffee house, or a park. Make yourself comfortable and write until you feel you've gotten your emotions down on paper. It may take several times to complete this process. If you can stay with it, the benefits are worth it.

After you complete the letter, release your feelings with a burning ceremony. Throw the letter into a fireplace or bucket and burn it. This will help you let go of the past and allow you to begin to accept your life as it is.

~ Anger and Resentment
I'm angry that I have cancer.

~ Hurt
I am sad that my life will never be the same.

~ Fear
I am afraid that I will die.

~ Remorse, regret
I am sorry this had to happen to me.

~ Wants
I want to live.

~ Love, compassion, forgiveness, and appreciation
I appreciate what I have.

My Healing Letter

MY HEALING LETTER

MY HEALING LETTER

My Healing Letter

MY HEALING LETTER

There is healing in releasing your anger. It helps move you forward toward a sense of acceptance. Whether you find your own techniques or use the ones that have helped me, I encourage you to apply them on a regular basis.

Here are some other activities you might try to get rid of the hostility that is making you miserable and suppressing your immune system.

Recognize: Know It!

Research and understand every fact of your diagnosis. Know all your options. Being informed is powerful.

Consult your medical team for reliable information.

Actualize: Do It!

I encourage you to physically release the tension in your body caused by your anger. Free yourself. Scream at the top of your lungs in the car or into a pillow, stomp your feet, hit some golf balls, or pound a punching bag. Maybe a good cry is what you need.

What action can you take right now?

Verbalize: Say It!

Tell your family, friends, and medical team how mad you are. Articulate your anger with someone, even if you have to express it to your pet!

Write down a few phrases that describe how you feel. Share your *feeling phrases* with a loved one, friend, or your medical team.

Here are some examples:

I'm an emotional yo-yo!

I'm a time bomb ready to explode.

I'm a pressure cooker ready to blow up!

I resent what has happened to me!

I hate feeling out of control.

PRIVATE THOUGHTS

PRIVATE THOUGHTS

PRIVATE THOUGHTS

PRIVATE THOUGHTS

Positive

Positive

Positive

Positive

A pessimist sees the difficulty in every opportunity, an optimist sees the opportunity in every difficulty.

—Sir Winston Churchill

I Want to Be Positive, but I Feel So Negative

Right after my diagnosis, a friend said, "Find the opportunities in cancer and live those opportunities with passion." How can you take an ugly situation, like cancer, and turn it into something positive?—especially with all the doom-and-gloom statistics. Was my friend suggesting that I find opportunity in adversity? If so, how do I turn lemons into lemonade?

After many months of bitterness, negativity, and anger, I discovered the secret—opportunities arise from an attitude of acceptance. Take what you have, deal with it, and adjust to it.

Cancer brings each of us a different gift, opportunity, or awareness. One person might receive the gift of opening his or her heart in a relationship; for others, it might be new career opportunities, and for someone else, it could be the need to eliminate stress. You choose to accept cancer, deal with it and move on, or stand still. By accepting the challenge and evaluating your life, you open new possibilities. Your courage in accepting your challenge sets an example for others touched by this disease.

What are the lessons you can learn from cancer? Can you look at cancer as an opportunity to evaluate your life? To look ahead and discover new life passions, which will make a difference in your life and others? This story illustrates how I turned a setback into a comeback and gave back.

For forty years, I lived my life without passion. It appeared as though I was living the ideal life. Raised in a wonderful family, graduated from college, married to my college sweetheart, living in a dream house in Santa Barbara, owning and operating a successful bed & breakfast, eighty-four steps from the Pacific Ocean. To the world around me, it all looked great, but it didn't feel great! I felt a void inside, which I tried to fill with material things, social status, and money. I surrounded myself with prominent people who drove the finest cars—"beautiful" people. I was hung up on my physical appearance. I couldn't hop in the car to run an errand without spending an hour primping. Heaven forbid if someone would see me dressed for working in the yard. It's hard work keeping up an image.

Eventually, reality bites back. I couldn't keep up this plastic facade. The inevitable happened. My life was torn apart, leaving me jobless, homeless, penniless, and cancer-stricken. Standing in the unemployment line, I asked myself what was left to live for. Lost and discouraged, I finished my business and drove to the ocean for a walk on the sand. It was then I desperately prayed for help and guidance. I knew I had two choices: I could check out or fight for my life. Right then I had a revelation: Fight for your life. A warm tingle filled my body, and, in my mind, I saw a light at the end of a very long dark tunnel.

At that moment it gave me peace, but things didn't automatically turn rosy and wonderful. There were many days I wondered if I was going to earn enough money for my next meal or rent payment, as I struggled to survive each chemo treatment. I was alone and afraid. Many nights, I lay awake as thoughts raced through my head. Was I doing the right thing by taking chemo? Would a man find me attractive, or was I damaged goods? Were there other women who survived my kind of breast cancer? Was I going to die?

These and many more thoughts, fears

and questions arose. I did have the support of my family, but they did not live near me. They phoned, mailed letters and cards of caring. My sister, Marilyn, a breast cancer survivor, was an invaluable source of hope. Her constant calls gave me courage to fight my battle. But what I desperately needed was a place of help and support in my own town: a drop-in center where I could find others who faced similar concerns.

My doctor told me there were other breast cancer survivors seeking the same thing. In November of 1996, a task force led by the renowned surgeon and author Dr. Susan Love, along with local care providers, physicians, and survivors, envisioned a resource center. I dedicated my time, along with other cofounders, to establishing a place where no woman scared, petrified, and overwhelmed with a diagnosis of breast cancer would be alone. These courageous women now have a place to go or call and hear a survivor say, "I understand how you feel."

Out of my tragedy, and the tragedy of others, came the birth of the Breast Cancer Resource Center of Santa Barbara. Collectively, we took our cancer experiences and turned them into a center that makes a difference in many women's lives and those of their loved ones.

Turning a Negative into a Positive

Can you remember a time when you took an ugly situation and turned it into something positive in your life? I encourage you to write out what happened.

Can you look at cancer as the beginning of a new life, instead of looking at it as the end of your life?

No one expects you to smile about your illness, but what about the new things in life you have come to appreciate, enjoy, or reflect on?

Can you think of positive benefits that you might never have come to appreciate before your cancer diagnosis?

Here are some examples: Watching the sunset, taking your children out for ice cream, giving a prayer of thanks for the meal on the table or the roof over your head.

Visualize these moments and jot them down here. Come back to these pages when you need positive support.

Take all the time you need to complete this activity. I promise you, you will begin to see the beauty in an ugly situation.

POSITIVE BENEFITS OF CANCER

Take Action

What small step can you take today toward accepting and seeing the positive aspects of your cancer? You might start out by repeating aloud these affirmations: "I am a survivor." "I am living each day as if my life had just begun." Speak with conviction and meaning. Feel strong; take ownership when you speak. Step into the space of receiving your cancer. And when you are ready—raise your arms and shout your affirmations. It may feel strange at first, but if you practice, you will begin to feel comfortable.

Or you might want to find a verse of thanks and repeat it daily.

Experts agree it takes 21 days to replace an old habit with a new one. So pull out the Post-It notes again with those empowering words, phrases, and quotes, and stick them up on your "Affirmation Wallpaper." Repeat these positive affirmations every day until these words fill your soul.

I challenge you to see the positive aspects of your cancer.

Unleash yourself from negative thoughts, which hold you back from realizing the possibility that new life opportunities await you.

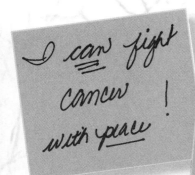

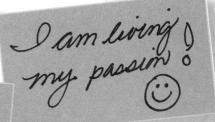

As I put words to my thoughts, these deep feelings had a place to go on the page. My mind was free of negative clutter, making room for positive healing images.

How do you feel today? Check off the words that jump out at you on the "Feeling Words" list (page 82). Circle at least five words that you feel strongly about and on pages 83 and 84 fill in your feeling word with the following journal jumper phrases:

I am feeling . . .

I want to feel . . .

What can I do to feel . . . ?

Here's an example of how I used the journal jumper phrases:

I am feeling exhausted because I'm doing everything myself, all my daily tasks. These daily chores don't stop because I'm sick.

I want to feel energized to have the vitality to enjoy life and not be dragged down by household chores.

What can I do to feel energized? I can start by asking others to help me with some of my daily tasks.

FEELING WORDS

Sad	Afraid	Magnificent
Angry	Sorry	Beautiful
Frustrated	Worried	Lovable
Disappointed	Scared	Overworked
Loving	Appreciative	Apprehensive
Grateful	Happy	Cared For
Peaceful	Courageous	Passionate
Exhausted	Confused	Blissful
Hysterical	Frightened	Regretful
Ashamed	Depressed	Sympathetic
Overwhelmed	Hopeful	Optimistic
Lonely	Lovestruck	Paralyzed
Jealous	Bored	Joyful
Shocked	Anxious	Misinformed
Despair	Distracted	Fantastic
Ambivalent	Betrayed	Isolated
Confident	Cherished	

Complied by Beverly Kirkhart

How Do I Feel?

How Do I Feel?

PRIVATE THOUGHTS

PRIVATE THOUGHTS

Who?

Who?

Who?

Who?

*It takes two
to speak the truth —
one to speak
and another to hear.*

—Thoreau

Whom Can I Talk To?

Prior to the opening of the Breast Cancer Resource Center, I felt isolated and undesirable. I desperately wanted someone that I could talk to—someone who would listen and understand my fears and concerns.

I had been healthy all my life and had no use for support groups until cancer struck. Cancer was the challenge of my life, like Mt. Everest is to a climber, deadly and frightening. However, most climbers who have successfully reached the summit were not alone on their journey. For me to survive, I joined a support group. I had read that people who join support groups tend to live longer and experience a better quality of life. You feel normal when others who know how you feel surround you. In a Stanford University study of women with breast cancer, those who took part in an emotional support program lived about eighteen months longer than those who didn't.

I encourage you to find support. It may consist of two, ten, or a hundred family or friends, individuals you trust and whom you call to express your fears, needs, and wants. Your support team might be a cancer group in your community, members of your church or synagogue, your medical team, co-workers, or an online support group. Consider joining a cancer quilting club or art therapy class. Your team offers a helping hand, a listening ear, loving words, and believes in you and inspires you to be a survivor.

Spend time finding your ideal group. I encourage you to attend several in order to observe their meetings and determine which fits your needs. I found my perfect match by getting very clear about what I wanted from my group. I visualized the members listening attentively and smiling, and I heard their words of hope and courage. My personal journey to find a support group was life saving.

On the evening I was first diagnosed, it was 2 a.m. and I was still awake, alone and frightened by my thoughts. What did the doctor say about my tumor? How would my body respond to chemo? Was there an alternative to chemo and radiation? Most

Wide Web chat rooms, all resources from which I could seek information. But they didn't fit my vision of a support group.

At this point in time, the Breast Cancer Resource Center did not exist. I realized I needed to share my experience face to face with others. I wanted to hear from other women survivors how they dealt with the loss of a breast, infertility, and the uncertainty of being cured. I needed

---

"Through my support group, I learned more what to expect, and the risks and benefits of certain therapies." — Jessica

---

everyone I knew who had this disease had died—my mother, grandmother, uncles, and aunts. Would I?

As I struggled alone, I wanted urgently to find others who faced similar fears and concerns. I found the local chapter of the American Cancer Society, National Cancer groups, and 1-800 numbers to the World

to learn how they survived and how they learned to live each day to its fullest with cancer. I was hungry to hear their inspirational stories. Doctors can treat the tumor, but it is stories from survivors that treat the soul.

The Santa Barbara community, my hometown, does a wonderful job in assisting cancer survivors and caregivers. I attended several hospital and community groups, but none of them satisfied my appetite for a survival environment. One evening, out of sheer frustration, I sat down and wrote a list of criteria for a support group. This process helped me to clarify what I needed and wanted, and it allowed me to select the group that would best meet my needs and expectations.

Twelve weeks after my diagnosis, I found my support: a group of five positive, loving, and supportive women, each facing different types of cancers.

Our insightful and loving facilitator, Rebecca, a trained counselor as well as a cancer survivor of twenty-seven years, guided us!

We met once a week at the same time and place. The meeting format was consistent. Rebecca opened the session with a moment of quiet reflection and an inspirational verse or story, followed by individual share time. Each person had a designated amount of time to freely express her issues, concerns, or thoughts.

"Get to a support group as early as you can. Don't be afraid—no one understands our thoughts and our fears better than one who has experienced it."

—Bonnie

We ended with positive acknowledgment of one another. If time permitted, Rebecca discussed exercises that addressed topics such as communication, goal setting, living a balanced life, asking for support, and life after cancer.

*"I surrounded myself
with people who believed
in me and reached out
to them for the courage
I was lacking."*

—Beverly

This group was empowering! I learned from these women how to survive. Their heartfelt sharing helped me become more playful and expressive. Thanks to their encouraging words I learned how to ask for what I needed and wanted, and how to live in the moment. They helped me rediscover the gifts within me. I learned how to appreciate my life from them. These brave and heroic individuals helped me to discover my personal journey to survival.

My mother, in her wisdom, found survival tools that allowed her to have a quality life. Just seven years prior to my diagnosis, she was told she had colon cancer. I observed from the sidelines her painful surgeries, treatments, and eventual slow agonizing death. But during her battle she never complained, lost her faith, or became discouraged. She was heroic and courageous.

I remember her saying to me, "Bev, what I need from you is a listening ear, a willingness to ask, acceptance of my choices, and endless love." During that time, little did I know some years later I would be fighting my own battle with cancer, using my mother's knowledge to rally my support team.

My Ideal Support Group

How would your ideal group look? There is value in each support group. Don't reject a group because it doesn't meet all your criteria.

Consider the following list of questions to help you write out your list:

Do I want to be in a group with people my same age?

Do I want the members of my group to have similar diagnoses?

Are the members good listeners?

Do I feel free to express my anger, fears, and other emotions?

Is the group positive, upbeat, and hopeful?

Does a skilled facilitator lead the group?

Is there a bond with the other participants?

My Ideal Medical Team

Your medical team is a vital part of your support. Consider the following questions as you develop your team of physicians.

Are my doctors qualified?

What are their reputations?

How do they listen to my needs?

How supportive are they?

Are they open to my suggestions?

How do they treat my loved ones and friends?

Who Can I Ask?

Can you remember a time in your life when you asked for support, when you needed that helping hand?

Take a moment and reflect on that troublesome situation. How did you feel when asking? What was your reaction to the response? How did the support person behave? Write out your thoughts below.

As patients we may not want to bother others, so we don't ask. But by not asking, we may be depriving others the joy of giving care. We can gently guide our family and friends to give us the practical support we need. We don't have to take this journey alone. People want to help but we have to help them to know how!

Asking for support from others was a difficult task for me because I've always been the caregiver. I put the needs of others before my needs, until a wise friend in my cancer support group told me, "the person who asks for support is the wiser, healthier, and stronger person." Her words sank deep into my soul; I realized I couldn't face cancer alone. Cancer was bigger than me. I would have to get support, which meant I had to ask. Little by little I turned to my loved ones and began to ask for what I needed and wanted. I spoke up and asked for help with meals, paying my bills, household chores, driving me to treatments, assistance with medical research, and much much more.

"He who asks is a fool for five minutes, but he who does not ask remains a fool forever."

—Chinese Proverb

Positives

Negatives

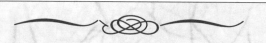

Why Won't I Ask?

Do you want to ask, but won't? What prevents you from asking? What are the benefits for you if you don't ask?

What chances or opportunities might you have missed in your life by failing to ask: Can I? or Would you? or Is she/he?

Write down the positives and negatives to asking someone for help—how will you feel, how will they feel.

My hunch is that when you have finished, the positives will far outweigh the negatives.

Go ahead and ask, because sometimes the answer can change your life!

My Lifeline to Support

Lifeline to Support

List ten things that you need help with. (This could be meals, babysitting, a question-and-answer session with the doctor, transportation to your treatments, health insurance, etc.)

Circle your most immediate need.

Who can help you with this?

Write out that person's name.

How are you going to ask them? *In person, by phone, fax, e-mail, or letter.*

When are you going to ask them? Day, month, time.

Be specific with your request. What supportive action do you want or need from them?

PRIVATE THOUGHTS

PRIVATE THOUGHTS

PRIVATE THOUGHTS

PRIVATE THOUGHTS

You gain strength,
courage and confidence
by every experience
in which you really stop
to look fear in the face.
You must do the thing
you think you cannot do.

—Eleanor Roosevelt

My Hero Within

A hero, as defined by Webster, is "a human being of great strength and courage; any person admired for his qualities or achievements and regarded as an ideal or model." As a cancer survivor, you have earned the title, bravely fighting your cancer battle and blazing the way for others.

Unfortunately, many of us don't recognize our strengths, realize our courage, or have enough confidence in our abilities to overcome our fears. Like the Lion in the *Wizard of Oz*, we think we are without courage. Often it's not until we are faced with a traumatic experience that we begin to discern the depth of our strength and determination.

During the most desolate time in my life, it would have been easier to turn away from my fears rather than face them.

But I didn't. I was willing to explore my feelings. I discovered a tiny flicker of hope burning inside of me. The fuel of hope was an affirmation I repeated each morning: "Today, I'm one day closer to the light at the end of the dark tunnel. I choose to live. I'm worthy of good health, happiness, and prosperity." These hopeful words gave me the fortitude to tackle my cancer challenge.

I now understand that when you are faced with tragedy in life, you have a choice: to find the hero within, or give up. By choosing to uncover your own courage, strength, and determination, you become a role model for others.

This is my "Hero Within" story:

While going through my cancer treatments, I met a friend who was going through similar treatments. We began to talk about what brought us joy, happiness, and personal satisfaction in our lives. One thing that we had in common was our love for bike riding. After sharing cycling stories, we realized that we should bike not just for enjoyment but to reclaim our lives. Both of us had been poked, jabbed, and prodded, examined like objects, and we had had enough! This is when I signed up for my 100-mile bike ride, The Century Ride.

I began training just six months after my last chemo treatment. Physically it went well, but I could not get past my own self-doubt. I had never done anything physically challenging, even when I was healthy.

To overcome my negative self-talk, I wrote out positive affirmations: "I can cross the finish line." "I can ride 100 miles." I also asked my family, friends, and medical team to support me with words of encouragement or supportive acts. When my bike broke, someone loaned me hers. When I was on a high carbohydrate diet, my friends brought me bowls of pasta.

Ride day came, a cold windy September morning. The route began in California's Central Coast at San Luis Obispo, then headed north on Highway 1 to San Simeon. As we turned onto Highway 1 and headed north, I hit severe head winds. I felt like I was riding a stationary bike—pedaling and pedaling, but getting nowhere.

I was thrilled but exhausted when I reached the 50-mile mark. After a short lunch break, I got back on my bike and headed south. I felt strong and in control. But as the miles clicked away—60, 65,

70—my back began to scream. Every body part ached, including a few I didn't know I owned. But I painfully kept in motion as I came upon the 90-mile mark. After 7½ hours in the saddle, I was filled with dismay. Directly ahead of me loomed a mountain—a *big* mountain. This was the mountain I had to climb in order to reach the finish line. How was I going to conquer it? I was near collapse. I just wanted to get off the bike and hitchhike home. It was at that moment of desperation that all the months of preparation, and all the support of my friends, flashed before my eyes. "I can cross the finish line," I told myself. "I love this challenge." With the voices of my friends, family, and medical team cheering me on from within, I put my bike in its lowest gear, and standing on my pedals I stubbornly inched my way up the mountain.

As I flew down the backside of the mountain and crossed the finished line I knew that I was my own hero. I was a survivor. I had summoned the courage to reclaim my life. There was nothing I couldn't handle now. I might have lost my marriage, my money, and temporarily my health, but I hadn't lost myself.

You have the potential to become a hero.

What does it take? The following are some of the characteristics. Some of these qualities are more easily developed than others, yet all require some degree of courage.

～ Hope for a positive outcome

～ Passion to survive

～ Willingness to look at adversity as opportunity

～ Readiness to take risks

～ Ability to speak the truth

～ Clear vision

～ Belief

～ Optimism

My Champion Moment

Can you recall a time in your life when you had a champion moment? A time when you set a goal and reached it? Sometimes we find powerful and transforming experiences in the simplest of things, like saying I love you to someone.

MY CHAMPION MOMENT

As a woman facing cancer, I fought every day with my self-esteem. I worried that others saw me as a bald lady, with no life and no future. At a self-esteem seminar, I learned an exercise called the Strength Wheel. I decided to use this exercise to test my theory.

Give this exercise a try. I guarantee your self-esteem will increase. Have your family, friends, co-workers, and support team fill in your strength wheel. You won't be sorry you took the time to get their feedback! Sometimes other people see our strengths more than we do.

Tape your strength wheel to a wall or door where you will see it every day, so you can be reminded of your greatness.

This exercise gave me an awareness of how I affected and enriched the lives of others. This was a Yes! experience.

My Strengths

In the inner circle on the opposite page, write down what you see as your best qualities, such as compassionate, dependable, friendly, lovable, trusting. In the outer circle, ask your family, friends, co-workers, and medical team to write down what they observe in you and what they like about you.

Make several copies of the blank strength wheel that you can give to others to fill in.

My Strengths

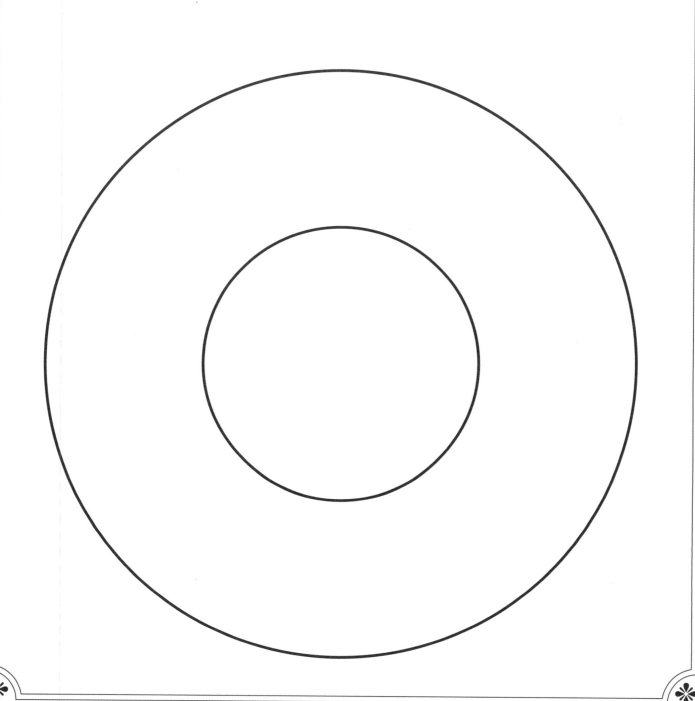

PRIVATE THOUGHTS

PRIVATE THOUGHTS

Hear

Hear

Hear

Hear

Kind words
can be short
and easy to speak,
but their echoes
are truly endless.

—Mother Teresa

Doctor, Can You Hear Me?

Communicate, communicate, communicate when talking with your doctors. Freely share your thoughts and feelings to promote understanding between you and them.

Expressing emotions to my doctors was difficult for me. My parents taught me to respect and not to question authority. Doctors were authority, so for most of my life I was too intimidated to communicate. That all changed after my diagnosis, because I needed more than medical jargon from them; I wanted to share my thoughts and fears.

My life was abruptly thrown into the medical world after I was diagnosed. It was shocking to be treated like a case study, as though I were a diseased object. During the early rounds of doctor appointments, I could not help but think about the Golden Rule, "Do unto others as you would have them do unto you." It seemed so simple for my doctors to treat me as they would want to be treated. To my dismay, I discovered that some doctors didn't know how to be gentle and compassionate, but I still had to make them listen to me.

Of course, not all my doctors were insensitive. I had a few who treated me as a person, with respect and admiration. To them, I say thank you for being patient in answering all my questions, handing me a tissue for my tears, and offering me words of support.

You might ask how I overcame my shyness with my doctors. It happened when I joined my cancer support group. I learned how to be assertive. One particular woman named Diane really showed me the way.

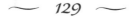

Diane was facing a second occurrence of ovarian cancer and searching for alternative treatments to shrink her tumor. As she discovered rare treatments or products, which might possibly reduce the tumor, she would without hesitation consult her doctor.

Their relationship was honest, open, and respectful. Her doctor listened to her. In fact, he told her that he appreciated her research and openness in sharing these alternative methods.

Secretly, I felt jealous of their relationship. Finally, one evening, I opened up to the group and spewed my frustrations and unhappiness with one of my doctors.

What I gained was good advice from a cancer friend. "Bev, you have to demand, take charge, and ask for what you want," Diane said. "This is your body and you are the one who knows your body the best. Listen to it! Ask your doctor for time to discuss your questions and concerns. Let him or her know that you want to be heard. And by all means talk about the support you need."

Simply stated, this is your cancer and you are employing them to cure it!

After listening to my group's heartfelt thoughts, insights, and suggestions, I made a commitment to stand up for myself and be heard. I deserve to be treated as a person and not as a diseased *object*!

Prior to my next appointment, I made a list, with help from Diane, of what I wanted to discuss with my physicians. By organizing my thoughts, I found the courage and took charge, asking my doctor to please listen. It turned out great. I created a warm, personable, and mutually respectful relationship with my doctors. I encourage you to take charge. You can do this too. If you find this difficult, consider bringing a friend or family member along to convey your needs. This second person can also help interpret the doctor's prognosis and recommended treatments.

Take Control

You may have a story in mind of how you took control of a situation and got what you wanted by speaking from your heart. As you write out your story, remember you can apply the same principles to your relationship with your doctor.

Communication can be extremely difficult when you have just been told you have cancer. I was frightened—so scared that I couldn't talk or ask questions, too nervous to tell my doctor that I didn't understand much of what he was saying. It also didn't appear that the doctor understood my questions. I had to learn how to ask and how to listen to his response. I learned by making ice cream sundaes with a friend!

Ice Cream Sundae Activity

This activity will help you learn the fine art of communication: how to ask questions, listen attentively and purposefully, and give explicit instructions.

What you need: ice cream, chocolate sauce, cherries, nuts, whipped cream, ice cream scoop, bowl, two spoons.

Instructions: Sit back to back with a friend. One person is seated in front of a table. The other person calls out detailed instructions on how he or she would make an ice cream sundae.

When you are finished, you may be surprised to find how differently you prepare a sundae from your friends. And how your interpretation greatly affected the results.

P.S. Yummy! Eat the ice cream sundae before it melts!

Communicating with Ice Cream

My Needs and Wants

Speak Up—Become Your Own Advocate!

Make a list of what you need and want from your doctor. It will help you to clarify your requests. When finished, practice aloud asking for what's on your list or brainstorm your questions and concerns with a friend or family member.

(A friendly reminder: Be respectful of your doctor's time.)

Here are some questions you might consider asking your doctor:

⁓ **Who can I talk to who has gone through my same diagnosis?**

⁓ **Is there someone who can help me navigate through the diagnosis, treatments, and beyond?**

⁓ **Who should I consult for a second opinion?**

⁓ **What is the recommended treatment for my disease? Is this standard?**

⁓ **What are clinical trials?**

⁓ **What side effects are there to the recommended treatment?**

⁓ **Where can I find more information about my cancer?**

⁓ **What cancer side effects best respond to complementary therapies?**

⁓ **What lifestyle changes (diet, exercise, rest) do you recommend I make to best manage my disease?**

⁓ **Are there activities I should avoid that may make the symptoms worse?**

⁓ **If new symptoms arise or existing symptoms worsen, what do you recommend I do?**

⁓ **Who should I call with questions or concerns during non-business hours?**

———— •– ————

Helpful hint: Read your journal entries to your medical team. So often when I tried to describe my symptoms and feelings about my situation, I became inarticulate, and I felt like I'd messed up. But when I read my entries, I was able to pinpoint my concerns. The power in doing this was that these journal entries conveyed the exact symptoms, side effects, and emotions I had experienced at a certain moment. What was impossible for me to recreate in spoken words was already there on the page.

———— •– ————

PRIVATE THOUGHTS

PRIVATE THOUGHTS

PRIVATE THOUGHTS

PRIVATE THOUGHTS

PRIVATE THOUGHTS

PRIVATE THOUGHTS

PRIVATE THOUGHTS

Hugs

Hugs

Hugs

Hugs

Hugs

We need 8 hugs for love

10 hugs for maintenance

and 12 hugs for growth.

—Virginia Satir

Hug Me!

*H*ugs are about realizing the importance of being loved, touched, and cherished. A hug is a simple gesture of affection that can bring tremendous joy.

I didn't understand the benefits of a hug because I was hugless most of my life. It wasn't until I began my chemotherapy treatments that I found myself starving for physical connection, especially from my doctors, because they were a vital part of my survival. I demanded hugs from them!

It is possible that in the midst of your treatments, you will miss what is really important. You may fail to tell your doctor, a loved one, friend, or caregiver that you need a hug. You may also be more likely to miss opportunities to give hugs.

Hugs come in all shapes and sizes, and from all ages and genders. Some of us are huggers, some of us are not. If you've never really been a hugger you may not know what you're missing. If you are a hugger, are you getting and giving enough hugs to keep you feeling loved? Don't be afraid to give hugs or receive them. At the end of each day ask yourself, how many hugs have I given or received today?

Here's my story: I was the patient who needed a hug, and I needed a doctor who would give me that hug . . .

One day, I was late for one of my endless doctor's appointments. I had to fight for a parking spot so that I could rush to a place where I had no desire to go. Once inside, the nurse called my name as if I was next in line at the meat counter. Once I got into my "private" room, I entered another unreal space. As usual, the examining table was hard and the room was small, colorless, and sterile. The gown I was given was limp and barely covered my private parts. (Right now you are probably nodding your head saying, "I can relate to this.") I sat alone in the cold examining room waiting for what seemed like hours for my doctor to enter. It was then I realized that the nurse didn't call my name to buy meat. I was the meat! I was placed in this room to be poked, prodded, and examined.

I said to myself, today things are going to change. The doc rushed in and gave me that quick medical glance, then read my charts as he gave his usual greeting. You know, "Sorry I'm late, let's see . . . hmm. . . how are your blood panels looking today?"

I'd had enough of being treated like that! I EXPLODED!

I said, "Look at *me*, ask me how I'm *feeling* today. Listen to me and most importantly, greet me with a hug!" To say he was surprised is an understatement. Quite honestly, I don't think he'd ever imagined such a thing before.

That day changed his life and mine forever. He looked at me, asked me how I was feeling, and stopped to give me a hug! From this moment forward our relationship shifted. Over time, he gave out hugs to others with great and unwavering enthusiasm.

Put Your Heart into Your Hugs

Are you hungry to be appreciated, respected, and understood by your doctors? Do you want compassion from your medical team—a loving embrace, handshake, or pat on the shoulder?

Hugging Instructions

Visualize hugging your doctor in this way:

Place the left side of your face along the left side of his or her face. Pull him or her toward you and give a big squeeze.

Imagine the caring, compassionate, and spiritual energy that is being transferred between you. Hugs bring you heart to heart with your doctor.

My experience taught me that it was okay to ask my doctor or anyone else for a hug. That day was a huge empowering step in taking back my life. I know you too can gather up your confidence to ask. Speak from your heart. It will change your relationships on all levels.

If you're not a hugger, it may seem awkward at first, but make a date with yourself to hug your doctor. What do you have to lose if your doctor doesn't respond? You have much more to gain! So go ahead, put your arms around him or her and give a loving, heartfelt squeeze.

One more thing—don't limit your hugs to your doctor. Spread the wealth around! Give out hugs to your family, friends, counselors, hairdressers, neighbors, whoever!

Congratulations! You have taken a big step forward in asking for what you want and need. Be proud of yourself! Hurray!

Remember, never forget to acknowledge your courage.

The Hug of My Life

Write in your journal about a special hug you received. How did it make you feel at the time, and what comfort do you gain today because of that special hug? You might title your story "The Hug of My Life."

My Hug List

The simple act of hugging is immensely powerful. You pick up and transfer energy to and from the person you're hugging. Write down whom you should be giving and getting hugs from every day.

For every person you have listed, you have probably forgotten at least three more.

MY HUG LIST

Alternatives to Hugs

If hugging is not comfortable or appropriate, try:

Placing your free hand on top of a handshake

Softly touching the person's shoulder

Rubbing the bald head

Giving a loving smile

Looking into the eyes of a person when talking

Winking an eye

Giving a thumbs up

Making a high-five sign or giving a hand slap

Any small gesture that sends a message of caring will go a long way…

PRIVATE THOUGHTS

PRIVATE THOUGHTS

PRIVATE THOUGHTS

Blues

Blues

Blues

Blues

Happiness is a butterfly,
which when pursued,
is always just beyond
your grasp, but which,
if you will sit down quietly,
may alight upon you.

—Nathaniel Hawthorne

What Can I Do with the Blues?

*D*o you wonder if laughter and playfulness can ever be part of your life again? The answer is a definite yes; you can turn a disheartened attitude into playful consciousness.

You might not feel like laughing, smiling, or being playful at this particular time. It's difficult to be happy when life has dealt you a bad hand. You may be asking yourself, how can I find happiness when my days are consumed with doctors' appointments, treatments, tests, surgeries, discussions about death, and horrifying cancer statistics?

I understand just how you feel. I didn't see where happiness could possibly fit in my life at the time of my diagnosis. In fact, I remember one evening when I was with a group of friends having dinner and I jealously thought, why am I with these people who find humor in life, when I might not even be alive in six months? Today, I look back and I think, what a morbid thought that was!

Laughter, humor, and playfulness are important tools for recovery, along with hope, the will to live, faith, positive thoughts, determination, and love. All of these factors working together give you a better quality of life, and with that comes the will to live.

Numerous studies have been done which show that laughter and a positive attitude can be healing. According to a study at Loma Linda University, after 30 minutes of laughter the medical students' disease-fighting white blood cells increased by 25 percent.

Knowing the benefits from laughter, I encourage you to discover ways to bring humor into your life. Let life entertain you! Many of our hilarious moments come from situations that happen to us personally. These funny moments might have taken place when you were a child, teenager, or adult. Dig into your memory bank, pull them out, and jot them down in this book.

Read these funny situations before you go to sleep. Your warm fuzzy stories can help to ease your mind of the troubling thoughts that creep into your subconscious at night and keep you awake.

I'm forever laughing at myself for the ridiculous situations I seem to get myself into. Let me share one such situation.

Monday was going to be a hectic day, meetings back to back. As I headed out to my first appointment, I noticed my car was almost out of gas. I pulled into a gas station that offered a free car wash with a fill-up. Looking at my watch I saw I was ahead of schedule, so I made the choice to take a few extra minutes to drive through the car wash. Sitting in my car, my mind wandered off into a dream world. I wasn't there long before I felt a rush of water soak my head and body. I immediately realized that I hadn't closed the sunroof in my car and water was pouring in. In the nick of time, I cranked the roof closed just as the water was returning for the rinse cycle. Drenched to the bone, I drove out of the car wash looking like a wet noodle and feeling stupid and embarrassed. I drove to a pay phone and explained my predicament to the client. As I was sharing, I found myself laughing hysterically—it hit me, how crazy I must have looked sitting in my car soaked. Find the humor in your situation and laugh at yourself.

My dear friend Elise, a cancer survivor herself, taught me a lesson in humor. Elise was always full of surprises, jokes, and funny stories. I looked forward to my support group meetings because I

> **Happiness does not necessarily come in the form of humor, funny stories, or jokes. It can manifest itself in the simplest of things—gardening, painting, playing the piano, tennis, or walking on the beach.**
>
> **Whenever I got the blues, I would try to immerse myself in something I knew would lift me up.**

knew Elise would have us in stitches as she told yet another one of her comical experiences.

One evening our group was discussing the issue of doctor-client relationships. Elise, who had a rare form of uterine cancer, jumped into the conversation with her story.

After many weeks of researching what her best survival options were, Elise reluctantly elected surgery to remove the tumor. She did her homework, and learned everything about her inner organs and their relation to one another. She said, "If I must have this operation, then I am definitely going to have a say in how the doctor is going to cut me open." She was an accomplished artist, a take-charge kind of woman who lives her life with a spirit of playfulness.

The night before surgery, she checked into the hospital. It was quite late and all lights were out—except in Elise's room. She plugged in her spotlights, attached and adjusted a mirror to a light pole so that she could have a clear view of her abdomen. She arranged her paints and paint brushes and carefully began painting a road map on her abdomen—explicitly directing the doctor around her intestines, liver, and kidneys. Upon completion of her masterpiece, she cleaned her brushes, put the furniture back in place, and turned off the lights.

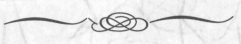

Give a Party

This is a unique party, where friends and family bring items that remind them of you—gifts they feel are symbolic of you. For example:

Teddy Bear
You are soft and cuddly.

Star Stickers
You are a "star" in their eyes.

Bubble Maker
You are fun, lighthearted.

Sugar Cookies
You are sweet and yummy to be around.

Heart Box
You hold their love.

Magic Wand
You are a magical person.

When morning arrived, Elise was fast asleep as a dozen doctors, nurses, and orderlies rolling with laughter abruptly awakened her. Gradually, she remembered her artistic masterpiece and joined in the laughter. Her only regret was that she wasn't awake to see the faces of the doctors and nurses when they first spotted the road map. She could only imagine that their expressions were worth the effort.

Elise shared her gifts of humor, laughter, and spirit of playfulness with everyone near her and it helped lighten the air around all of us.

Let your friends and family members lift your spirits. You will be inspired by the feelings and the heartfelt affection of your loved ones. This gathering promises to be fun, playful, and filled with laughter!

Celebrate your ability to create playfulness, joyfulness, happiness and laughter into your world.

Your Joy List

What do you do that makes you happy? List those things that bring you joy and delight. If reading Elise's story brings to mind a humorous situation you have experienced, write it down. When you are finished, take a moment to enjoy your memory!

My Joy List

Gettin' Rid of the Blues

In your ideal world, what can you do with the blues?

What can you do right now for a belly laugh?

Whom can you call for those funny jokes?

What movie can you rent?

What hilarious story can you share about yourself?

Whom can you ask to help bring out the playfulness in you?

Where can you go to be playful?

What can you do to bring out the kid in you?

Write down your ideas and review your list. What steps will you take right now to brighten up your life?

You might consider other types of journals to help keep your spirits uplifted.

The following are some examples.

~ **Humor journal**

~ **Gratefulness journal**

~ **Joyful memories journal**

~ **101 things you want to accomplish**

~ **Prayers of appreciation journal**

~ **Dream journal**

~ **Inspirational quotes**

PRIVATE THOUGHTS

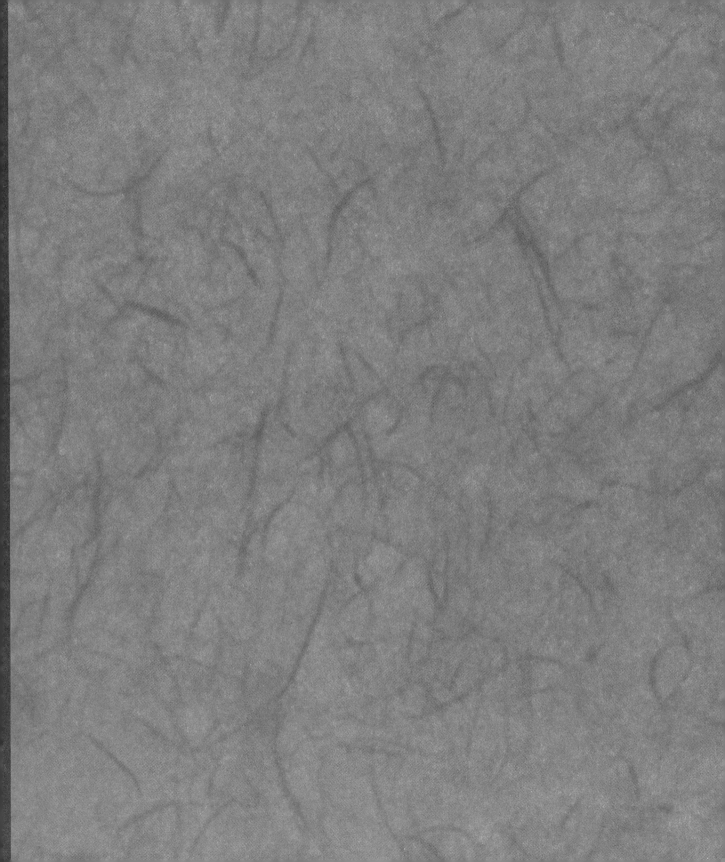

Beauty

Beauty

Beauty

Beauty

*I love to give
and receive gifts,
but I know that
the greatest gift I have been
given is my self.
I am a beautiful reflection
of a loving Universe.*

—Louise Hay

Mirror, Mirror, on the Wall

*Y*our beauty lies within. Have you ever met someone who wasn't the most good-looking or beautiful person in the world—yet, because of their demeanor, warm style, and confidence, they radiated a beauty beyond their personal appearance? These individuals understand that there is more to life than good looks.

I learned this lesson at the lowest point in my treatment—looking in the mirror and seeing my bald head. Both my hair and my husband were gone. I didn't feel feminine, beautiful, or desirable. I was humiliated, embarrassed, and angry. People told me that being bald was traumatic, but your hair isn't who you are, and besides it grows back.

Women who had lost their hair suggested that I find a way to soften the blow. "Take charge," I was told. "Don't wait for your hair to fall out, shave it off!" People prepared themselves for the loss of their hair in many different ways—saving strands of hair for bird nests or celebrating the loss with a hair cutting ceremony. I know husbands, friends, and caregivers who shaved their heads in solidarity.

I took the advice of others who had walked this hairless road, and I honored my process by cutting a piece of my hair and gluing it into my journal. There was value in honoring my hair; it gave me a method to grieve the loss.

I, too, would recommend that you do not wait for your hair to fall out, but find someone who can shave your head! This action will give you a sense of control. However, I don't think anything can be done to prepare you 100 percent for the shock you will experience when you first look into the mirror and see your bald head. For those of you who have joined the no-hair club, you understand what I am saying. But those who are about to be hairless, I don't mean to frighten you with my honesty. My intention is to help you face reality, move through your fear, and take this opportunity to see that your beauty is not in your hair— it's in your soul. I never had the courage to go outside in public with my bald head. Instead, I wore all kinds of colorful scarves in a variety of shapes and sizes. I would creatively wrap and tie the scarf around my head with a fashionable hat. This was my way of turning a traumatic event into something playful and innovative.

Truth be known, I would have loved to walk around town with a bald head exposed. I admired the individuals who could freely show off their shaved heads.

Not only did they have guts, but everyone of them looked beautiful.

My wish came true on Halloween. I was invited to a costume party held at the local contemporary art museum. Knowing exactly what I wanted to do, I called Elise, my artist friend, who was thrilled to participate in my fantasy. On Halloween day, she went to work and drew a whimsical design on my upper body. She painted my hairless head bright orange and drew an elegant face so it looked as though I was wearing a masquerade mask. I stopped people in their tracks! Partygoers came up to me all night long, rubbing my head, only to discover the orange headpiece and the mask were painted on. All night I proudly responded, "Yes, I have no hair!"

"Your beauty is not in your hair—it's in your soul."

As a result of being bold and BALD, and stepping out of my comfort zone, I felt a sense of freedom. I discovered my beauty was not in my physical appearance but inside me.

I encountered a mirror exercise in a workshop led by Jack Canfield, co-author of the *Chicken Soup for the Soul* series. This powerful exercise gave me the strength to see the beauty of who I was without hair. I invite you to try this activity. I promise you, if you do this simple exercise for 21 days, your mind will automatically shift from the negative self-image to seeing yourself in a positive view as the wonderful, beautiful person you truly are.

Mirror Exercise

Who's the Fairest of them All? I Am! I Am! I Am!

Every morning or evening, look yourself in the mirror and acknowledge your best qualities. Say something like, "I am a loving, compassionate, friendly, giving individual." (Review your qualities you wrote down in your Chapter 5 Strength Wheel.)

When you have finished, end with, "I Love You." Be sure to hold eye contact in the mirror and express these words with meaning and sincerity. I Love You—these are three powerful words when you are blind to your inner beauty.

Surprise!
Beyond My Physical Appearance

Can you recall an occasion where you had to get beyond your physical appearance through the mere act of being who you are? For example, maybe you've experienced a horrible perm job or bad haircut. How did you respond to this dilemma?

What did you gain from this predicament? Whatever story you come up with, write it down. You'd be surprised at what you may have learned about yourself.

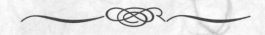

BEYOND PHYSICAL APPEARANCE

Reflections of Me!

Take time out of your day and rummage through your photo boxes or albums (if you are that organized). Find childhood pictures that make you smile. Glue your photo memories on these pages.

R E F L E C T I O N S   O F   M E

**Fun Things to Do
with Your Bald Head**

Have a hat party.

Use it as a message board.

**Exchange wigs with people in your
support group.**

Paint it.

**Hold a beauty parlor party and
decorate each other's bald heads.**

Massage your head.

**Buy a variety of wigs in different
shapes, styles, and colors.**

**Drive in a car with a convertible
top and let the air tickle your bald
head. Don't forget your sunscreen!**

I support you in seeing the beauty that is in you right now, this very moment. Stand tall, be proud of who you are, AND don't be afraid to wear your inner beauty on the outside. Smile from the inside out —illuminate those around you with your beauty.

"I love looking at myself in the mirror. I view myself without judgment, seeing only a beautiful spiritual being with a unique appealing body."

— Louise Hay

Bald is Beautiful ... Unfortunately I never realized this until years after my treatments. Looking back, I have a list of regrets that I call my bald head wish list. In sharing, maybe you can embrace these wishes to help you celebrate your beauty.

∼ I wish I had taken tons of pictures of myself—bald.

∼ I wish I'd worn different colors and styles of wigs.

∼ I wish I had let my family and friends see me bald.

∼ I wish I had worn big outrageous earrings.

∼ I wish I had surprised others by pulling off my wig.

∼ I wish I had let people rub my bald head.

∼ I wish I had attended the American Cancer Society's program "Look Good, Feel Better" to help me with my appearance while undergoing treatments.

PRIVATE THOUGHTS

PRIVATE THOUGHTS

PRIVATE THOUGHTS

PRIVATE THOUGHTS

PRIVATE THOUGHTS

Let the beauty
of what you love,
be what you do.

—Rumi

Finding My Joy

Your life is FOREVER changed by cancer. What does that mean? We all have our own personal interpretations. For me, it means: Having stared death in the face, my life is a precious commodity. I now live life with a newfound appreciation, gratefulness, and respect.

Cancer is a wake-up call for most of us. It shakes us up in different ways, but the bottom line is that we need to evaluate our lives. Are you living your life to its fullest potential? Are you using your God-given gifts?

When cancer struck, I felt as though I was standing in the middle of a suspension bridge. Everything behind me was burned to the ground, and ahead of me was a blanket of dense fog, the unknown. Did this fog represent death? Or did I have a new future in a career, relationship, family, and financial security?

My choice was to remain fearful —stuck in the middle of the bridge—or to take a step of faith and move toward an unknown future. I elected to trust the unknown. I took steps forward, believing I would see a beacon of light, a path of new opportunities through the fog that surrounded me.

As I took those faltering steps, people began to show up in my life in many different ways. I met mentors and teachers who gave me books to read and encouraged me to attend lectures and workshops. I enrolled in adult education self-improvement courses and the Women's Economic Ventures program, and joined the Self-Esteem Council. I was like a sponge, soaking up ways to live a fulfilling life. I networked with new acquaintances who had contacts, referrals, and a network base. These steps weren't easy, nor did they happen overnight. I worked hard to overcome my roadblocks and obstacles by staying focused, taking each day at a time and persistently moving forward. Doors of opportunity swung open with my association to the *Chicken Soup for the Surviving Soul* book. Slowly, the fog of uncertainty began to lift as my life led me into the speaking profession.

Cancer gave me the opportunity to change my life. It forced me to get out of my comfort zone, discover my true self, and go for my dream. Going after your vision can be tough.

Just months before my diagnosis, I was forced to file bankruptcy. I found myself standing in the unemployment line after losing my business. I had no idea, concept, or clue as to what I wanted to do with my life. I was overwhelmed with stressful thoughts: What do I do? What are my skills? Where do I go to get help?

How does one find a new job or career at 42 years of age? Am I marketable? The answers to my questions weren't simple or quick. I struggled to find the right tools that would help me discover my new path.

With the help of Margi, a successful career coach, I dusted off my dreams and asked myself what I wanted to be when I grew up. I remember saying things like, "I want to be a teacher, nurse, counselor, or parent." I wanted to have an effect on people—to make a difference in someone's life!

My college degree, skills, and training were in marketing, so I thought if only I could work on projects or products that helped people, this would be satisfying. To my surprise, it wasn't. After I was diagnosed, I realized my passion is to encourage, inspire, and motivate people to find what they love to do and do it. It was difficult to turn down paying clients in order to pursue an uncertain dream. Margi was instrumental in helping me clarify this vision. Together we identified my action plans and steps to reach my goals.

With her assistance, I made career choices rich in commitments to a new future.

Still excited and enthusiastic, yet frightened, I began to take the steps to become an inspirational speaker. I joined Toastmasters International and spoke for free to every civic group in my community. I took whatever opportunities came my way to share my story and deliver my message. I wanted people to know that cancer isn't a death sentence.

Opportunities present themselves at the appropriate time in many different ways, as I discovered when I met Jack Canfield, co-author of *Chicken Soup for the Surviving Soul,* at a self-esteem program.

Mr. Canfield was seeking a cancer survivor to speak at a kick-off event in Santa Monica. I jumped at the opportunity and before I realized what I had committed to, I was standing in front of 350 people in the Santa Monica Civic Auditorium telling my story. I was a featured speaker sharing the stage with a variety of celebrities. This was a quantum leap for my career. I was on my way.

I now have the privilege of traveling across the country, delivering a message of hope and inspiration to those touched by cancer.

Opening the Door to Happiness, Fulfillment, and Peace

Choosing to live with passion opens the door of life to happiness, fulfillment, and peace.

Write about a turning point in your life when you believed so strongly in something that you went after it with passion. Your passion was so strong it carried you through difficult times.

"Hold fast to dreams,

for if dreams die,

life is a broken-winged bird that cannot fly."

—Langston Hughes

HAPPINESS, FULFILLMENT, PEACE

Passion! Passion! Passion!

Take a moment and think about what you still feel passionately about.

Light candles, play your favorite inspirational CD, turn off the phones, put out the "Do Not Disturb" sign. Relax your mind with a few deep breaths. Do not self-judge and do not self-criticize. Let your imagination go. Write whatever comes to mind!

Reflect on the following questions: What lights my fire?

What would make me want to get up in the morning and shout, "I love my work and life!"

What is my ideal vocation if I were given all the skills and talents necessary?

If money was no object?

My Passions

MY PASSIONS

MY PASSIONS

Create Your Ideal Life Picture

Take a look at your ideal life and write the answers to these questions:

Relationships/Family
How would my relationships look in an ideal scene?

Health
What would my health be like in an ideal setting?

Spirituality
How do I envision bringing spirituality into my life?

Living Environment
How would my home look in an ideal setting?

Financial
What would my goals be in my ideal setting?

Recreation/Play/Hobbies
How would I spend my free time in an ideal setting?

MY IDEAL LIFE & FUTURE DESIRES

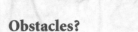

Obstacles?

List potential obstacles to hinder your ideal life:

What major obstacles might you encounter?

How is your cancer and its treatments likely to get in the way?

What proactive steps can you take to ensure you are moving in the right direction?

ACTION TO REMOVE OBSTACLES

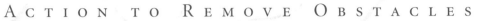

"Future Desire" List/Ideal Life   **Potential Obstacles**   **Action Steps**

Collage of Your Ideal Life

Are you ready to have some fun with this idea and be creative?

I encourage you to bring your written list into conscious awareness by creating a visual display of your ideal life. Make it into a collage of images on a white 22" x 28" mat board.

You will need magazines, a sturdy clean surface, mat board, glue sticks, and a pair of scissors.

Cut out words and images that represent your ideal life and glue them to a poster board. Have fun creating it.

Share Your Desires

Take your passion and dream ideas and your ideal life picture and collage to a loved one or trusted friend. Review your dreams, visions, thoughts, and ideas with him or her. Ask for feedback. Sharing dreams with people who support and believe in you can trigger insight and bring about additional creative ideas.

Seeing your dreams written out stimulates your thoughts and makes them real. Sharing these written dreams enrolls loved ones in your vision and often leads to new and exciting possibilities.

"The Future belongs

to those who believe in

the beauty of their dreams."

—Eleanor Roosevelt

PRIVATE THOUGHTS

PRIVATE THOUGHTS

PRIVATE THOUGHTS

PRIVATE THOUGHTS

PRIVATE THOUGHTS

PRIVATE THOUGHTS

PRIVATE THOUGHTS

Live Today for Tomorrow

Congratulations on completing *My Healing Companion*. You have accomplished quite a task. Be proud of your achievement and by all means, acknowledge the commitment you have made to your self-growth.

I hope you have discovered while writing in *My Healing Companion* a safe place to express your deepest heartfelt feelings. You found the stories and exercises healing, offering hope, courage, and peace with your cancer. You rediscovered the beauty that lies within you and a burning passion to live your dream. Joyfully you recognize your God-given gifts and eagerly look forward to sharing them with those around you. There is no time like the present to let your greatness shine.

A new chapter in your life has emerged with cancer. From the moment you were diagnosed with this disease and each day that passes, you are a survivor. You've learned how to live for today and have hope for tomorrow, finding the confidence and courage to bravely face the future and its opportunities that await you.

You are a role model for those who are to follow in your footsteps. In confronting your adversity, you offer hope to others that they too can discover there is life after cancer. No matter how great or how small your act of kindness is in giving back to others doesn't matter. What does matter is that you will offer hope and courage to those facing their cancer journey. Please join me in making a difference by shining a light of hope on those touched by this disease.

I wish you the best of health, happiness, and success in making a difference.

God Bless You, Beverly

From Beverly: Thank you to all of my Angels

When I began to create this journal, I started out with an idea that I thought would help others like myself who have been touched by cancer. All along the path to making this book a reality I came across and was touched by angel after angel. At every corner or turn, someone unsolicited came into my life and gave of themselves and their love to this book. As you make this journal your own, you need to see the names of these people and know that they too are part of this healing companion. Know that their healing energy has been infused into each and every one of these pages.

Thank you, all.

Mark Alciati	Suzanne Fox	Gerd Jordano
Melonie Alciati	Debbie Frazier	Jim Brennen
Aunt Ruby	Terri Frank-Cross	Karen Brennen
Roy Arnold	Anna Friederich	Lynne Cage
Patty Aubery	Rick Harrison	Jack Canfield
Dianne de Avalle-Arce	Stan Hatch	Steve Cashdollar
Ruth Bach	Mark Victor Hansen	Kim Christiansen
Paula Bass	Beth Higgins	Marilyn Clem
Carey Berkus	Judith Hill	Shel Clem
Deborah Breedon	Hal Hollister	Mark Clem
Jill Eickenberry	Janet Hollister	Susan Clem
Linda Ellerbee	Melissa Hollister	Pete Jordano
Teresa Esparza	Wendy Huntley	Cindy Iliff

Fredrick Kass, MD

Gail Kearns

Dr. Susan Love

Julie Main

Peg McCormick

Rebecca McLean

Margi Mainquist

Alixe Mattingly

Marcia Meier

Nancy Mitchell

Mom

Terri New

Issy Patton

Cindy Peer

Christine Pickett

Katie Clem

Alexandra Clem

Peter Clem

Jacque Clem

Riley Clem

Cynthia Daddona

Nina Dall'Armi

John Davies

Bob Demetriou

Eldon Edwards

Kelli Ringrose

Gail Rink

Paul Roberts

Jeri Rovsek

Richard Rovsek

Dr. Bernie Segal

Dad and Louise Smith

Julie Spenser

Arlene Stepputat

Camille Staley

Amanda Staley

Volunteers @ BRC

Martin Walker, MD

Judi Weisbart

Ron Whately

John Wigel

Vince Wong

Jennifer Worick

Marilee Zdenek

These Are My Angels

On the following pages, list all of your angels past and present. You may ask, when will I know that an angel has come into my life? All I can say is: you *will* know, and when that angel comes, list that person or pet and acknowledge his or her charity.

MY ANGELS

M Y   A N G E L S

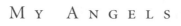

M Y A N G E L S

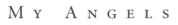

M Y   A N G E L S